the EVER-LOVING ESSENCE of YOU

CREATE A LONG-TERM CONNECTED RELATIONSHIP
WITH YOURSELF

JAMIE LERNER
&
LAUREN TARG

ISBN 978-0-6153-4819-3
Library of Congress Control Number: 2010922186

Published by: A Tangerine Dream
1555 N. Sheffield Ave.
Chicago, IL 60622
info@atangerinedream.com

Authors: Jamie Lerner & Lauren Targ
Edited by: William Atwood
Graphic Design: Melissa Palmer Atwood

May you always follow
your inner knowing

Peace & Love,

Jon

Acknowledgements

We would like to thank our editor Will Atwood and our graphic designer Melissa Atwood. It was a pure intuitive decision to ask Will and Melissa to work with us. Their gentle coaching and great design sense has contributed immeasurably to this joyous experience.

We would also like to acknowledge our family and friends for supporting this endeavor and being part of our life experience.

HOW THIS BOOK CAME TO BE

The relationship we have with ourselves is singularly the most important relationship that we will ever have. In every life there is a moment of clarity when you know your inner being is calling you, and the only choice you can make is to listen and go with it. That moment of clarity is the inspiration for this book.

I was born with a knowing; a true sense of who I came forth to become. My inner voice was always clear. Along with this sense of knowing, I was sometimes confused when it came to understanding my relationship with my mother. Here was this marvelous creature who I felt emotionally disconnected from.

As a small child I remember wondering, how could I be so completely connected to my true self, and yet be so disconnected from the very person who gave birth to me? I have spent half my life trying to figure this out. My incredible mother felt the need to immerse herself passionately into the world. She was deeply and completely involved with numerous international organizations, causes, and philanthropic foundations. It seemed to me that she appeared the happiest when she was "saving the world." As a result, I believed that if I were just a little more interesting, more intelligent and more beautiful, then she would see me, and we would become connected—I would become a part of her.

I had one of the most fantastic, interesting, and somewhat surreal childhoods. I was a product of the '70s, when life was about redefining one's self, one's family and one's country. It was a wonderfully freeing and confusing time. I grew up in a family where we were encouraged to explore and embark on each and every amazing opportunity. My mother was engaged in the spirit of the times, enjoying her new freedom and lobbying for the freedom of all women, children, and the disenfranchised.

Our house was a revolving door of interesting people from all over the world, along with their many causes, missions, hopes, and dreams. From political activism meetings and huge international dinners to independent small artists and theatre groups, our family hosted them all. My mother was at the forefront, passionately and relentlessly creating possibility for change and spinning dreams into reality.

We were "free to be" in every sense of the word. I was in the midst of it all, and yet I could not see where or how I fit in. Only later, as an adult, after having children of my own, was I able to clearly reflect upon the beauty of my early years with curiosity.

In essence, I lived in a parallel universe; wanting emotional connection, but not at the price of personal freedom. I remember looking at my family, and, although we were all co-existing as a family unit, I felt total disconnect occurring for me in the household. With that observation I had a moment of absolute clarity. I had to be true to myself at all costs, even if it meant never having the connection that I always dreamed of having with my mother.

From my earliest memories, I was always looking to do my own thing—just following my own inner being. I was never the popular girl and always the trendsetter—way, way, way before the trend. Life for me was always about answering to myself, and I was impossible to influence. I was 12 years old, running wild and free, and exploring all that was out there. I ran fast and played hard, searching for the path of least resistance in every opportunity presented to me. I was popular to myself and always beat my own drum. I knew myself well and had the freedom to express it. It was the '70s, a time of redefining everything. It was *my* time.

My parents were on their own extraordinary path. While my father ran his corporation, my mother, with five children at home, was out trying to change the world. When she was not out creating change in the world, my parents were traveling the world. We were cared for at home by the most interesting array of people, from nannies, to international exchange students, to missionaries. Each and every one of them quickly became a part of our family. My parents always felt that if we could help make a difference in someone else's life, then why not? It would certainly make our own lives richer.

So everyone was given the same wonderful messages of encouragement as I: "Find your passion, follow your passion, be open to knowing and learning as much as you desire. Life is full of endless opportunities, and if there is a will than there is a way." My parents lived their entire life by these principles.

My teenage years were a time of seeing and experiencing the world. With my parents' ongoing encouragement and support, I traveled to Peru, Guatemala, spent a summer in Israel, and camped in the Sinai dessert with the Bedouins. We were encouraged to seek out and satisfy our every curiosity. I was fascinated by people from every culture, always wanting a greater understanding of the dynamics of their interpersonal relationships. I found myself very interested in the study of psychology, and knew that I would go on to pursue that as my major in college.

Throughout my life, I never questioned the love that I felt for my family, and I always felt their love for me. However, I continued seeking out an emotional connection with my mother, wondering what that would feel like. My mother was very involved in her own passions, and so I was left to check in only with myself. They endorsed and paid for all of my adventures, and I felt their approval. Even if they didn't understand what we were doing, they supported it with their spirit of love and enthusiasm. Yet my mother was not available to emotionally connect with me. This perplexed and bewildered me. There was always someone present in our home, but it was not my mother.

My incredible mother approached all aspects of her life with almost supernatural energy, enthusiasm, and intensity. She believed that there were 48 hours in every day. She lit the candle at both ends, and in every way lived the lifetime of ten people. She was her greatest strength, and she was her greatest fear. She sidestepped the most important relationship; the one that she had with herself.

It was not until she was admitted into the ICU in January of 2009, after a 15-year struggle with scleroderma (which she had so gracefully concealed from all of her friends and colleagues), that I was really able to feel the connection with my mother. She was placed on a breathing tube and heavily sedated to keep her pain-free. I sat with her for days, finally feeling as though I had my mother's undivided attention. I talked to her about everything that we had not talked about for all the years of my life as her daughter. For the first time I found her to be completely in alignment with herself and at peace. As I felt the love pour through her, I kept thinking that maybe this was the beginning of our wonderfully connected relationship as mother and daughter.

My mother made her transition to non-physical five days after this special time I spent with her. I remember feeling so complete and connected, knowing that she had finally been given what she was wanting, and had been sidestepping the entire 75 years of her life: a connected relationship with herself.

In a small, beautiful, round box I carry the

ever-loving essence of my mother. I take her everywhere with me, knowing that she would want to be part of my every adventure. I talk to her day and night, and I feel her presence around me like a blanket of warmth, love and deep connection.

I came to understand that my lack of emotional connection with my mother had to do with one thing and one thing only, and that was her lack of emotional connection with herself. I now know I could not have picked a better mother for myself.

I would like to thank her for allowing me to know myself, and for allowing me to find my true self when I was lost. This book is offered in appreciation for all the contrast my mother provided me, and with the knowledge that without her I may never have been so clear in my connection with myself.

Jamie Lerner
Barrington Hills, IL, 2009

CONTENTS

-LOVING

ESSENCE of YOU

WELCOME

It is our belief that people are amazing and beautiful. They are filled with light, love, passion, joy, and enthusiasm. We are beings with intuitive knowing and infinite intelligence. We can learn anything, can have everything, and can manifest well-being in our lives.

And sometimes we get stuck.

Stuck is a moment in time. Yet it only takes a moment to make a shift to a better-feeling place. This book is filled with powerful tools to assist you in making that shift. This is far easier than it might sound. Most often it is not the situation itself that has created the misalignment, but it is how we *feel* about the situation. How do we change the storyline to create a better feeling place to move forward to? Sometimes we simply need permission to redirect ourselves inward, back to the most important relationship, the one that we have with ourselves.

It is possible to achieve a happy, healthy, and prosperous life that you can live every day. How can we make that shift?

Think of a time when you are standing or sitting, and you make a subtle movement to get more comfortable—you are making a shift. People do this all the time, everyday, intuitively knowing how to make themselves comfortable. This represents the simplicity of making a shift. You can also create this subtle process in your mind. It is a little nothing, and yet it is everything. We will often refer to making a shift throughout this book. It is important to understand that this subtle movement can be done with ease.

We invite you to be gentle with yourself. For some of you, these concepts will be new, while for others they will be gentle reminders of what you already know and apply on a daily basis.

This book has been written in a way that allows you to navigate as you wish. You can read it from beginning to end or simply read the parts that feel good to you. We hope that you find *The Ever-Loving Essence of You* an inspiring book, and one you can carry with you and refer to at anytime.

YOUR INNER BEING

Your inner being is a small voice that is always guiding you. You can choose to tune into it or not. It is a constant; your inner being never tires, never punishes, and never abandons you. When you tune into it, it is like coming home. It is your guiding light of love and acceptance and connection to yourself in the most joyous way. Your inner being is on call 24/7, 365 days a year, just waiting for you to tune in and be guided. It is your personal Jesus, your Buddha, your Abraham, your grace, your Krishna, your guru, your Bodhi, and your Al-Mahdi. It is your personal, private assistant who will never call in sick, never judge you, and never turn an unkind eye to you.

Your inner being is your biggest cheerleader, your ongoing support system who has your back—and the backing of the entire universe.

It is free, and it is yours until the day you make your transition into non-physical. It is the ever-loving essence of you.

What are some of the ways for you to connect or tune into your inner being? For everyone it is different. One way to help you make that connection is to create a small opening in the conscious part of your mind. Pause from all thought and slowly count to twenty. This will allow you to turn the volume down from your mind chatter. Mind chatter is the ongoing conversation that your unconscious mind is having with your conscious mind. In Buddhism, they refer to this as the mind of the drunken monkey. This is because the mind chatter is disorganized and creates a feeling of complete chaos. It is as if we are completely distracting ourselves by our own thoughts.

Usually, we are unaware of the content of this conversation, and it becomes the soundtrack of our unconscious mind. But when we become aware of our mind chatter, we are then able to turn the volume down and listen for our inner being and our guiding voice. Sometimes we need to give ourselves permission to redirect inward, and to become reacquainted with that small voice. At first, this might feel a little bit awkward. Some will recognize this guiding voice immediately, while others will take a little longer to tune into this small voice. Be patient and gentle with yourself throughout this process.

It feels so good to know that you can and will be guided by your inner being. Trust yourself. No one can guide you better than your own inner being.

When you are lost, just turn on your internal GPS (global positioning system), and allow yourself to be found by your higher being. Your inner being is the part of you that is completely connected to source energy — or, in other words, your higher being. Just slow it all down. Start with your mind, then your heartbeat, and then with a calm and deliberate voice, soothe yourself by reminding yourself that "you're fine, you're fine, *you are fine*." Talk yourself down enough to be able to hear your inner being. You have the answer, whatever may be occurring. Look inward, and know that help is on the way. You are the help, and you are going to allow your inner guidance to take you to wherever you need to go. You know, you know, *you always know!*

Feeling Good

Sometimes we just need to give ourselves permission to feel good. Feeling good has nothing to do with outside circumstances. The connection with ourselves is what gets us back to that feel-good place that so many people have practiced themselves away from.

We are all born with a knowing, a true sense of who we are, and an innate sense of well-being. We throw ourselves into the mix of life, and the contrast helps us decipher our desires. We are continually given the message to look outside of ourselves and to please others with our behaviors and actions. We are asked to measure ourselves based on others' ideals and the standards of society. It is essential that once we look *outwards,* that we then look *inwards.* It is only then that we can consciously assimilate all of the solicited and unsolicited feedback in such a way where we ask ourselves, "*how does that make me feel?*"

If the situation you are in feels good, then it is resonating with your inner being. If it does not feel good, then it is not resonating. You can then refocus your attention to something that feels better. Only you can do this for yourself. To do this is to continually look within and feel your way around all the data and stimuli and energy. You get to choose, as you selectively sift through your day, where to put your attention, based on what feels good to you. Trust yourself, and you will not miss anything that is important or relevant—if anything, you will have more clarity about what your questions are and where the answers lie.

Selective Sifting

Selective sifting is an important process that will allow you to refocus yourself back to your natural state of feeling good. Once you learn how to do it, you can apply it to any situation; whether it be watching the news, reading the newspaper, participating in a group conversation, or talking with members of your family. Soon you will be able to use this tool as you feel your way through your day. Selective sifting is a process (which can also be thought of as a practice) that encourages you to solely focus your attention on the parts of the conversation or the commentary that is pleasing to you.

When you use the process of selective sifting,

you are 100 percent present, and you begin to sieve through the content and information, only identifying the parts that resonate with your inner being. As a society we are drawn to the drama and sensationalism of every occurrence. Society and the media make us believe that we are to focus on the heightened events of the day. In reality, the focus on these events is what stands in our way of connection. If we allow ourselves to engage in the fear-based information which is readily available to us on a daily basis, we become paralyzed and unable to sufficiently process information.

The process of selective sifting is a tool that can be used every day, thereby allowing the connection to your well-being to thrive, as you move about the world in a productive way. When practiced 15 minutes a day, within 30 days you will sufficiently be able to apply this process to help you maintain your well-being.

When you are first starting to practice this

technique, it is best to begin by sifting through a conversation. Start by identifying the parts of the conversation that feel good to you, and only put your attention on those parts. An example of this might be when you are in a conversation with a colleague. Instead of talking about the work at hand, your conversation turns to gossip about another employee. Although this gossip may feel good to some, to others it might interfere with the good feelings that they had intended, or *pre-paved*, their day with. Selective sifting is an ongoing practice, and for some it may take constant redirection to focus on the positive. The reason for selective sifting is to maintain that good-feeling connection with ourselves.

Self-Trust

When you do not trust the voice inside you, you do not feel good. You can blame everyone else around you, or you can understand that you are, for the moment, out of alignment. This is a temporary disconnect. When you are irritable, depressed, or out of sorts, ask yourself, "what is it that I am using as my excuse to be temporarily disconnected from myself?" It is in those times that we tend to find blame with the world around us. We look to blame our partners, our government, our economy, our friends, and our family, when in fact the cause is simply us turning away from ourselves. Instead, we could ask: how can we get back to tending to ourselves and trusting in a way that allows us to maintain our loving connection?

Have you ever been in a situation when your inner voice was guiding you to do or not do something, and you chose to ignore it? When we choose not to listen to our inner voice, we often find ourselves in situations that are less than desirable. One example of those less-desirable situations could be as simple as driving your car and getting a feeling that you should slow down, even though there is nothing in front of you which would warrant such a decision. You get the feeling again, and still you ignore it, and then out of nowhere the car that was well ahead of you has slammed on the brakes, and you end up smashing into its rear end.

We often sense things with our inner knowing well before the hard evidence appears.

Another example: you travel for work and take the same flights week after week, and on one particular day you get a feeling that you should call and check to see if the flight is leaving on time. You look outside and see that it is a perfectly sunny day. And you dismiss the strong urge to call ahead and check. You then get to the airport and your flight has been canceled. You might say to yourself, "why did I not listen to myself?"

Day after day, you drive the same route to the grocery store without having to even think about it. On one particular day, for some reason, you turn left instead of right, and without really knowing why, you take a different route to the grocery store. On your way home, you realize that there was a car accident, which you would have been involved in, if you had questioned your intuitive decision to turn left instead of right.

Trust yourself. You know, even if you do not know how, or why, you know. For instance, you may have purchased a new home, and at the closing the voice inside you tells you that this is not the right place for you. Everyone is waiting to sign off on the mortgage. The agents are expecting to get paid, the lawyers are making sure everything is in order, and you might feel uncomfortable about letting your inner voice guide you to choose not to close. You might feel that because everyone has expectations of what is going to happen, you are compelled to move forward with the plan. When you get into your new home, there are problems with the structure and the neighborhood. If you had listened to your inner voice, then you might have had to rearrange some things, put your furniture into storage, and find a temporary place to live. But you would have given yourself more time to find a home that is better suited to you.

We have all heard stories about brides and grooms who knew that the wedding vows they were exchanging did not feel right to them. All the preparations had been made, the guests were there, and the gifts had been given. And the couple felt they must move forward, even though inside it did not feel right to them. If they had listened to their internal voice and stopped the ceremony, then they may have avoided an undesirable relationship that resulted in divorce.

We often hear from life partners who say they "knew" right away when they met their mate. Sometimes it doesn't seem like it is a match that could work—maybe it wasn't what they were looking for—but their inner voice told them to take the leap, and the relationship evolved into something better than they could have imagined.

Your inner voice also guides you to great rewards. It might be telling you to move across the country, even if doesn't seem "logical" or good on paper. You haven't figured out what you will do for work or where you will live, but when you get there, all the pieces fall into place. It feels like coming home to a place you have never been before. You easily find a home, work finds you, and you make friends effortlessly. Trusting your inner voice brings you fulfillment in ways that are beyond your expectation.

Trust yourself. You know what is best for you, even if you do not know how, or why—*you know!*

Your Inner Being   20

HAVE A LOVE AFFAIR WITH YOURSELF

The relationship we have with ourselves is singularly the most important relationship in our lives. The minute we are born, we feel an enormous amount of love pouring out of us, and reflecting back to us from our family. Then, as we grow, other people enter our lives. We experience more contrast. We are introduced to a myriad of thoughts and opinions that may or may not resonate with us. This can be confusing, and may contribute to the sense of disconnect we sometimes feel within ourselves.

Adolescence is a formative time in our development. It can be a very exciting and often bewildering time. It is a time of self-absorption, and a time to question everything. We are introduced to many new concepts and ideas about how we are "supposed" to think and behave. This often creates a disconnection with our inner knowing. In other words, sometimes we get stuck in a moment in time. During our adolescence, we create patterns of thoughts and feelings that we may continue to recreate in our adulthood. Some of these patterns may disconnect us from our inner being, inner listening, and inner knowing.

Other people have a point of view about nearly everything we say and everything we do. We often rethink how we feel about ourselves, based on those points of view. We are conditioned from day one to look outside of ourselves. Very rarely do we hear how important it is to redirect our attention inward, back to our natural state of connection. Society trains us away form our natural state of well-being and self-love. However, *The Ever-Loving Essence of You* is not a commentary about our society. Society provides us with a wonderful opportunity for contrast, and how we choose to assimilate that is up to us.

It is the most amazing thing that we have all of these experiences with society as young children, and then all of these choices about how to integrate them as adults. We can use these experiences as our excuse why we never go on to connect with ourselves, *or they can become the very reason for the connection that we create with ourselves.*

For example, if your parents divorced, you may be carrying some of the thoughts and feelings from that situation into your adult relationships. You can choose how you use that "devastating" divorce experience. One choice would be to never go on and create a healthy, loving adult relationship. Or you can use that experience as a wonderful opportunity for contrast, and the very reason to go on and create what you feel is the most loving, connected adult relationship for you.

The most important thing to understand is that you have choice: your choice to soar, or your choice to spend the remainder of your life arguing for your limitations.

What exactly does it mean to argue for your limitations? When suggested that we can re-frame our situation and make a shift, our tendency is to argue to remain where we are. This is what we find ourselves doing most often when we do not see an opening or possibility to move forward and thereby embrace a wonderful moment. We have become so invested in telling our story that we create resistance around changing the storyline, or we may simply need permission to change our storyline. It's all okay. Re-framing is a tool that can be used to look at a given situation and create an opening for a better feeling to move towards.

Self-love is an intrinsic part of our nature. Our

connection with our inner being is what gets us back to believing that sense of self-love.

We cannot love ourselves based on other people's point of view on how we should conduct our life. Wouldn't it be nice if we were not dependent on what other people felt about us to feel good about ourselves? Sometimes, other people are not reflecting our best selves back to us.

What are some of the ways that we can maintain the connection with our best selves and reflect it back to ourselves steadily, thereby creating and recreating the loving connection? The answer is, nourishing ourselves to connection.

Nourishing yourself to connection

The idea of nourishing and nourishment is different for everyone, but starts with the question: "what are some of the things that we can do for ourselves to feel good?"

You may be doing some of these things already, and not even recognize them. For example, your morning coffee could be more than just a jolt to get you going. If you put your attention on enjoying the ritual of your morning coffee and acknowledge the pleasure it brings, then it may set in motion the good feeling you want to move through your day with.

You could re-frame your morning coffee as something that brings you pleasure. If you are looking for the news of the day, another choice may be the great website called Gimundo.com, "good news served daily." Gimundo sets the tone for a loving, peaceful, connected, and inspiring world by providing information that you will not find anywhere else. It is mind-awakening and creates an automatic feel-good sensation.

Sometimes nourishing yourself is simply sitting quietly and breathing in the beauty of the morning light, as you listen for the birds chirping outside your window. If you live in the city, it may be taking in the beauty of the morning skyline, as it becomes the backdrop for the city's brilliant architecture.

Re-framing your experience of the day could be 10 minutes of stretching your body, or 30 minutes of gentle yoga. For some it is a vigorous morning run. You get to choose what feels like the best way for you to hook yourself up with you.

These few minutes set the tone for the day. It is saying "I am going to nourish myself before I nourish those around me." When we are nourished emotionally, physically, and (for some) spiritually, then we can extend ourselves in such a loving and unconditional way. It is giving with both hands. This unconditional giving often provides us with the most joyful feelings.

Pre-paving

Another powerful tool is called *pre-paving*. Pre-paving is a wonderful way to approach your day. It is a five-minute process where you allow your mind to take you through your day, exactly how you would like it to unfold, and how you would like to feel as it is unfolding.

Visualize, as you tap into the feeling of flowing through traffic and finding the perfect parking space, cooperative and harmonious interactions with everyone you encounter, anticipating wonderful service wherever you find yourself, and seeing and allowing every door to open for you. See yourself moving through your day with a deep sense of connection, appreciation, and joyful anticipation. Your mantra for the day is *"Everything is going my way."*

Each one of us has something that makes us feel good: whether it is meditating, taking a walk, climbing a mountain, cooking, tending to our creativity, or cranking up the volume of our favorite music. Ultimately, it does not matter what you choose; making the connection to yourself is what is most important.

How can we expect to have a love affair with another, if we have not created that loving relationship with ourselves? Without self-love we can not authentically love another. It is very important that we do not remain dependent on other people reflecting back the best of us. We need to do that for ourselves.

The ultimate hook-up is when you redirect yourself inward, to the connection that you have with yourself!

ALIGNMENT

The process of alignment is simple. It all begins with a conscious thought. Alignment is the process of adjusting parts so that they are in proper relative position.

The next step toward creating alignment is to line up the feeling with the thought to create harmony between them. Once you have achieved this balance, thus creating the alignment, you can choose to either take action or choose to not take action. You may be in alignment with one subject while still creating alignment with another. The beauty of this recognition is that you can create alignment with any subject matter at any time.

Alignment before action applies to everything that we do. In our work, in our play, attending to ourselves and others—it is a process that we encourage you to incorporate as much as you can into your daily living. We believe that no matter what the subject is, if alignment is created before action, the outcome will be fantastic.

When we are not in alignment, our connection to the most basic pleasures of life is lost. Instead, we have turned these pleasures into ways to manage our day-to-day frustration and anxiety. We often find ourselves using food, alcohol, and sex as a way to cope with stress. Our approach to these pleasures has been presented as illicit, clandestine, improper, and immoral. In other words, they have become "guilty" pleasures. How can we re-frame these activities so that we can reap the pure benefits of these pleasures?

When we are not in alignment with these simple pleasures, we sometimes find ourselves using these things to mask our feelings, instead of having a relaxing, engaged experience.

When we engage in these activities to heighten our existing, connected state of feeling good, these pleasures become ways to enhance our daily lives. Instead of using alcohol to block out the trials of the day, a nice glass of wine can complement your meal. Consider how you would like to feel before you engage in any activity. This consideration will create a connection between you and the activity and set the tone for alignment.

Let's look at some examples that everyone can relate to: eating, drinking alcohol, and having sex. You may feel confused by this list of examples, so let's take them one at a time.

Food

Food is a wonderful way to nourish our bodies. Meal time is a platform for a lot of our social interaction, and, for some, cooking is a hobby or passion. We as a society have a lot of confusion around food. What is one day proclaimed good for us is on another day contradicted. There is so much conflicting nutritional information about our food choices. We have lost touch with our connection to how we feel about our choices as we make them.

If we were to pause and create harmony between our thoughts and feelings about what we were about to eat, and with the food itself, then our bodies would be able to properly and peacefully metabolize our food choices, whatever they may be.

When we clearly and consciously allow ourselves to make food choices based upon what feels correct, and when we allow ourselves the pleasure of enjoying our food without conflict, worry, or guilt, then our food becomes a wonderful way to nourish our bodies and our minds.

It is never about the action that we take. It is,

however, about how we *feel* about the action that we take.

For example, if you have a sudden urge for ice cream, pause and ask yourself: "What kind of ice cream am I wanting, and what flavor would taste good? Would I like my ice cream on a cone, or perhaps in a dish with sprinkles? Where would I like to sit or stand with my ice cream? Would I like to eat my ice cream as I am walking down the street, looking in the shop windows, or perhaps sitting on my couch watching a favorite television program?"

Think about how good the ice cream will taste in your mouth, and the joy it will give you with each and every bite. Now you are in alignment with your choice to eat ice cream. You have created a loving peaceful relationship with the forgotten pleasure of something wonderful.

Your body can only use this dessert choice as nourishment. There is no misalignment here because you are not eating the ice cream to feel good, you are feeling good, and from that connected place *choosing* to eat ice cream. Ice cream enhances the good feeling that you have already created for yourself.

Libations

In the United States, people are not by law permitted to drink alcohol until the age of 21. We create so much mystery and taboo around the subject of drinking alcohol that once again there is confusion for us—especially for our younger generation. We have demonstrated, through our fear posed as concern, that if we incorporate alcohol in our daily meals with our children, somehow they will lose control and become alcoholics.

Drinking in this country is thought of as a way to relax, let off steam, and deal with stress. How many of us come home at the end of the day and wind down with a drink? This is usually our relationship with alcohol.

If we were to first create alignment with ourselves, lining up the feeling with the thought to create harmony, before taking the action of pouring ourselves a drink, then we would feel good. And from that place of feeling good, choose to either have a drink to enhance the already good feeling, or even skip the drink because we have accomplished, through the process of alignment, what we had expected the drink to do for us!

Drinking alcohol from a place of alignment enhances the already good-feeling place that you are in. On the other hand, drinking alcohol to create alignment does not work, ever. So once again, it is not the drinking of alcohol that is the issue, but the *feeling* about drinking the alcohol that creates the alignment or misalignment. The action becomes irrelevant.

In summary, we invite you to consciously create a good feeling within yourself before you set out to drink alcohol.

Sexual relations

We would like to offer this definition of sexual relations: sexual relations are the expressing and receiving of physical and emotional pleasure.

Of course, everyone will approach the subject of sex through his or her own individual thoughts and beliefs. Whatever your views may be, our belief is that the most important conversation to have with yourself about sex is that of being in alignment.

From a place of alignment with yourself, sex is the loveliest way to share with one another. It becomes the physical extension of our expression of how we feel about ourselves. That's right, sex is transformed into *the physical extension of our expression of how we feel about ourselves,* from our greatest point of connection with ourselves.

From a place of feeling connection with yourself (that is, loving yourself), you will only be attracted to and attract a partner who is also loving himself or herself. In other words, when you are in alignment with yourself about your sexual desires, then you will only attract a partner who is also in alignment about his or her own sexual desires.

The physical expression of two people coming together from a point of loving connection is the most perfect example of sex. It is enhancing and sharing yourself from a place of *already* feeling good.

Many people use sex to feel better about themselves. When you engage in sexual relations and want to sustain the good feelings, then it will be beneficial to begin from a place of alignment. Be clear with yourself that you are not engaging in sex to mask unwanted feelings.

When we align ourselves from a connected place with any subject prior to taking action, then the outcome will be fulfilling, satisfying, and pleasurable.

When we understand and embrace this concept, and then pass it along to our children, they can begin to understand sex as the loving expression of the connection that they have to themselves.

We often see young girls engaging in sexual behaviors early because they "just want to be held." What this really means is that they want to feel connection with themselves, and they believe that this can occur through sexual contact. Most of the time, this feeling that they were looking for is short-lived, if even momentarily experienced. But they have no basis for understanding why they are not feeling connected, so they try again and again — looking for love in all the wrong places.

It is a gift to encourage our children to fall in love with themselves first. It will then be through that alignment with themselves that they will seek out others who have also created that connection with themselves.

Romance

If your intention is to align yourself with romance, remember that romance is different from love. It is a state of mind. It is a feeling we can create around many subjects.

Most often we look for romance in our relation- ships. We usually look for someone else to create a romantic setting for us, but romance is also something we can create for ourselves. You can romance anything with, or without, anyone else around. Why wait for another to create romance in your life when you can experience it in your now?

When you give attention to yourself and listen to your inner voice, you can create a physical and emotional environment that is romantic to you. This can be a perfect platform for attracting a romantic partner; however, regardless of whether or not you have a partner, you can live a romantic life!

Inspiration

Inspiration is most often a by-product of alignment. When we are inspired and then take action, it usually turns out well, because we are in alignment with the task at hand. When you are in alignment, every action you take feels good. You are enthusiastic and feel like you are in a flow with yourself.

How can you tell if you are in alignment or not? This is best answered with an example:

when you know you have a work assignment that is due, and it's on your mind, the thought that "this is something that must be done" will persist. If you approach this assignment from a place of something that you "have to do," it will tend to create resistance within you. How can you align yourself to the task?

A powerful alignment tool is — surprise — *procrastination*. Resistance often leads to procrastination. Procrastination has gotten a bad wrap, and we are here to tell you otherwise.

Procrastination is a beautiful thing, because it reminds us to pause and take time to align with the action before we continue. It is important to recognize that when you are dreading doing something, then this is not the time to do it, even if you have a deadline. Embrace "procrastination is my friend" as your new mantra.

Sleep is also a wonderful way to release

resistance. It reminds us and allows us to get into alignment before we take inspired action. The Dali Lama said, "Sleep is the best meditation."

When we consciously put ourselves into alignment with anything, the outcome is successful and brilliant. Clearly it is the misalignment that creates the mishaps.

Once you understand the importance of alignment, and then understand the benefits of procrastination, you will learn that the only effective action is inspired action.

It is difficult to motivate yourself into alignment or to motivate yourself to take action. The only successful action is inspired action, or action from inspiration. When we feel inspired, we have lined up our thoughts and feelings, and the outcome of these inspired actions is magnificent. When you are ready to take action you will feel no resistance, and you will be able to move forward with ease.

For example, on the first of every month, you may not be feeling inspired to pay your bills — in fact you may feel some resentment. You have chosen to procrastinate and put this off for yet another day. Brilliant. You have now created the perfect opportunity to create a better-feeling relationship with this task. Use this as a wonderful opportunity to re-frame your thoughts and feelings around your bills. Take a moment to reflect upon each service that you have received and each purchase that you have chosen to make throughout the month with a sense of appreciation. This will help you set the tone for creating a good feeling around paying your bills. This may take practice. It takes 30 days to consciously change any habit.

Inspired action feels effortless. When we live by default, we create a life of default. When we live a conscious life of creation through thought first, alignment second, and action third, then it's sweet success every single time.

You can take any task and create inspired action around it. After you have created inspired action, it will no longer feel like a task. It will feel wonderful. Imagine every day creating harmony between how you feel and the activities of your day. Imagine setting aside all the drama, resistance, and resentment and instead taking inspired action. You will flow, flow, and *flow*.

APPRECIATION

Appreciation is a wonderful way to distract yourself if you are feeling disconnected and wanting to make a shift back into a connected state. It only takes a moment to redirect yourself to a place of appreciation.

Appreciation is the unconditional loving and allowing of ourselves, and the process of emanating, or *flowing*, that to others. Appreciation is a feeling that—once we call upon and allow ourselves to relax into it— assists us in recreating and maintaining the connection that we have with ourselves.

Appreciation is a state of being; in the loveliest way it reminds us of how good we feel when we remain connected to ourselves. We feel appreciation as we flow, feeling the connection to ourselves and others.

For one reason or another, we sometimes may find ourselves unable to feel appreciation, but wanting to. How can we bring this wonderfully powerful state of being back into focus?

Finding ways to tap into the state of appreciation is as simple as looking and feeling all around us. It could be catching a moment where the sunlight comes through the trees so beautifully, or holding a cherished gift. It could be a great song on the radio that makes the commute to work a bit more fun and gives you a chance to sing along. It could be giving yourself the gift of a delicious cup of coffee and deriving pleasure from the smell, taste, and feel as it warms your hand.

Appreciation is often just breathing in a loving moment of reflection. Once we understand how we can tap into appreciation to remain connected, every moment becomes a celebration: a celebration of yourself, a celebration of others, a celebration of everything.

Appreciation is a way for us to engage and indulge our senses as we milk a *wonderful* moment or experience, such as a meal, a memory, or a thought. We are surrounded by so much aesthetic beauty, and yet oftentimes we bypass the opportunity to indulge in the basking or reflecting of it all, as we go on with our day-to-day lives.

When we step out of our head and into our life, it is then that we are no longer simply going through the motions. We are now consciously attaching ourselves to our day-to-day experiences. Appreciation is a state of being that reconnects us back to feeling good, as it engages and indulges our senses.

When we begin a new relationship, or purchase a new item, or go on a vacation, it is easy for us to place our attention on what we acquire, or on our new surroundings, as we delight in the *wonderment* of every detail with a sense of giddiness.

For example, when we are in the early stages of a relationship, we indulge our senses by placing our attention on all of the wonderful details about the person — the way they look, the sound of their voice, what they say, where and when they say it, what they wear, how they smell, and the color of their eyes. We are wonderfully obsessed with every single aspect and detail of the person.

This is being in a state of appreciation. It feels so good to feel connected to ourselves, and the feeling of appreciation has taken us directly to this connection.

Purchasing a new dress or item of clothing may allow you to indulge your mind in the entire shopping experience, as you take yourself back to the moment when you saw the clothing in the window and entered the beautiful boutique or shop. Remember how you felt when you stepped into the dressing room to try it on with a sense of joyful anticipation. Reflect upon the friendly, helpful salesperson who made the experience of shopping so easy—the way she delicately hung the dress or clothing on a fine, wooden hanger, or the way she carefully folded it and placed it in a bag. This, too, is being in a state of appreciation.

We have so many wonderful opportunities to immerse ourselves in appreciation, even when we go to the grocery store. Whether it is the wide, easy-to-navigate aisles of the store, or the friendly, helpful customer service, focus on being in appreciation.

How about all of the splendid produce that glistens with the spray of fresh water as we hear the simulated roar of thunder before the rain? Imagine the bakery department, with the smell of fresh breads and desserts, or the flower section seen in most of our supermarkets, with its lovely array of bundled beauty. Breathe it all in with your senses and allow yourself to indulge in the feeling of appreciation.

Our car is where we spend a good deal of time throughout our day. Whether it be to carpool our children, or drive ourselves to and from work, our car can be a means to get from place to place, or it can be our beloved means of transportation. Your car is a cooperative component that you can rely upon for so many things.

When you get into your car, before you start the engine, give yourself a moment to settle into the experience. Consciously set your travel mug in its clever holder, take a moment to find a comfortable seat setting, and think about how wonderful it is to have such a reliable, safe vehicle to transport you and your precious cargo, day in and day out.

Use the experience of being in your car as a wonderful opportunity to tap into the good feeling of appreciation. Not gratefulness— this is something else. Tap into appreciation, where you lead yourself with your senses, not your feelings of guilt or worthiness. Allow your feelings of appreciation to wash over you because it feels so good.

Our pets provide an amazing opportunity for us to step into our feelings of appreciation. They model this for us all day long, because that is their natural way of being connected. Pets often unconditionally adore our every movement, as they shower us with appreciation with their untiring affection. We ourselves are also in a state of appreciation as we pour over our animals with endless love and affection. The very thought of interaction with our pets usually transforms us instantly into a state of appreciation and well-being.

We invite you to play this game with yourself. Take a moment and consider all of the people in your life. Allow yourself to identify one positive thing about each person. It could be something they say, or the way they smile, or perhaps their sense of humor, or any observation about them that you admire.

Whatever it may be, make it something about this person that inspires you and makes you smile and feel good. Now use this reference that you have identified, and only think about this one positive thing when the particular person comes to your mind.

This is a game which allows you to isolate something wonderful that you appreciate about each person in your life. It is a game that helps you shift your focus from an internal running commentary about each person to a condensed good thought/feeling of appreciation.

You will feel better, because you now have a positive, clear way of quickly thinking about the people in your life and feeling good. Vibrationally, that good thought/feeling of appreciation will connect you to yourself.

When we immerse ourselves into a state of appreciation and flow (these loving thoughts to ourselves and to others), it feels amazing. Appreciation feels like a blissful state of connection.

DELIBERATE
CREATION

Desire is defined as "an expressed wish or request." If we use this as our working definition of desire, then we can begin to understand it as the jumping off point of everything. Our desire propels us into the entire manifestation process.

Even though people are often uncomfortable speaking about what they desire, it is the basis of everything we have created in our lives. Some of us have been taught that it is not good, or that it is selfish, to talk about what we want for ourselves.

When we do not clearly express our wants and desires, we find ourselves living in a place of default, and often not satisfied with the life we are living. This is an opportunity to embrace what you desire in your life. Without the desire there can be no clear manifestation. Ask yourself the question, "am I living by default, or I am I creating the life that I live?"

We cannot want too much or have too much of anything. There is so much abundance out there in the world—enough for ten worlds, and available to all who tap into it.

How can we become the powerful, deliberate creators that we came here to be? In any moment, at any time, there are opportunities to deliberately create. In situations that you may have previously found frustrating, you will now have the tools to create an opening for manifestation.

Let's look at some of these opportunities. When you are in a car, on a plane, waiting in a long line, holding on the telephone to be connected to an extension, or any time when you are idle, use this time to create your every desire. While your first impulse might be to pick up your Blackberry™ or your iPhone™ and text a friend, we would like to offer another option for your consideration. Choose to put yourself into the head space that allows for flowing thoughts, by consciously releasing feelings of frustration about the waiting time.

If you are in a public setting, place your attention on something that is pleasing to you: a picture, a window, a person, or whatever allows you to feel good when you focus upon it. Take a deep breath and let it out, and feel your body relax into your natural state of well-being. We deliberately create with our thoughts. Do you know what you desire? No, really, *do you know what you desire?*

Bask in the appreciation of this moment, where you can focus upon something that you want to happen, or a specific desire that you have. You could also use this time to reflect upon something that makes you feel really good when you think about it.

Allow yourself to feel the relaxed state that you are creating in your body with thought. As you are doing this daydreaming, you are raising your vibration. Our good-feeling thoughts emit vibration that translates to the point of attraction. We are vibrational beings. Remember, we only have control over two things: what we think about, and how we feel.

The most important reason to raise your vibration is to feel good. From that good-feeling place, you can become a much more powerful manifester.

Oftentimes people who are dissatisfied in their job or current situation have the most wonderful opportunity to use the contrast to know what they do want, by knowing what they *do not* want. Let's talk about this as a possibility.

Throughout the day, re-create the job or situation that you want for yourself, simply by focusing only on the parts of the job or situation that please you. Most people may think that this would keep them in the unwanted job or situation, but this is not the case. When we focus upon anything wanted or not wanted, that is what we receive. So, if you want more of the good aspects of your job or current situation, then focus your attention on only those wanted aspects, and that is what you will receive.

If the workplace or current situation can only provide a little of what you desire, then know that a wonderful situation will come up for you — perhaps another job with more of what you are appreciating in your current situation. However, if all you have focused upon are the parts of your job or current situation that you are not wanting, then this is what you will receive. If your dream job or dream opportunity were to land in your lap, you would miss it completely, because your attention would be on the undesired, and not on the desired.

Let's explore the possibility of creating, or re-creating, an interpersonal relationship. If you are in a relationship now, you have a wonderful opportunity to create the relationship that you desire with either this person, or another. Begin by identifying and focusing only on the parts of your current relationship, or a past relationship, that feel good to you.

It can be as simple as identifying how your partner speaks, or perhaps dresses. You could focus on a single physical characteristic, like eye color, or a gesture that makes you smile as you reflect upon it. Your focus may even be how your partner whistles when coming through the door. Start with simple, small things that *please* you. Identifying the things that make you feel good about this person will not keep you there. To the contrary, it will help you create, or re-create, your desired relationship. What you think about is what you receive, so use this relationship to think about the things that please you, and you will surely receive more of those things from the person you are with. If it is not your desire to remain in this relationship, then you will have positioned yourself perfectly to attract someone else into your experience, someone who has more of what you do desire.

If you are not currently in a relationship, you can use this same process to create the relationship you desire for yourself, by focusing on the parts of past relationships that feel good to you.

Now let's explore the possibility of creating or re-creating a change in your body's condition. If you are feeling unhappy or dissatisfied by your current weight or level of fitness, and would like to create some changes, we suggest that you begin with deliberate creation.

First of all, it will be helpful for you to get yourself into alignment around your body and the views that you have about it. Not society's views or your friends' views or your family's views, but your own personal views. There are many people that feel really good about their body, until they open up a fashion magazine and believe that what they see is what everyone is supposed to look like.

Airbrushing and Photoshop™ techniques have created illusions around our beauty standards. Please understand that these standards only hold true for the fashion industry. Unless you happen to be a fashion model, we suggest that you revisit your own personal views about yourself, and how you would like your body to look and feel.

Take a few moments and consider all the things that you really like about your body, and how you feel *inside* your body. Isolate only the things that make you feel good as you reflect upon them. You may really love your thick, long, beautiful head of hair, or it may be the bone structure of your face, or your jaw line.

In great detail, delve into at least one thing about your physicality that you love.

Focus on the things you love as you go on to identify the change or changes that you would like to make from where you are. Once you are able to identify these changes, ask yourself if you can see yourself clearly in this new light. For some of you it will be about losing weight, for others it will be about toning and muscling up your body, and for still others it could simply be about obtaining a different level of fitness.

If, for you, it is about losing weight, then the conversation that you have with yourself could go as follows: "I really love the thickness of my long, beautiful hair as it drapes down around my shoulders. My hair frames my face in such a complementary way that it brings out my big, green eyes."

Now identify the change: "I remember how good it felt to slip into my favorite jeans."

Finally, create a feeling around that thought: "I felt sexy and confident in a way that only a great pair of jeans can make me feel. I can make a shift in my thoughts about where I am now and get back to wearing those jeans again."

You are now getting into alignment around this subject for yourself. You are lining up your thoughts with your feelings, and you are getting yourself ready to take inspired action. You will begin to recognize this as inspired action, because everything that you now do, for yourself, to create this desired change will feel easy and natural.

You, through the process of creating alignment around this subject, have created a clear and loving connection between your thoughts and feelings.

You are now, with great success, able to take yourself from where you are to where you want to be. This will not happen overnight, but every day your alignment with yourself around this subject will get you closer and closer to your desires. You may want to develop a mantra for yourself such as, *"every day in a relaxed and focused way I am creating the change that I would like for myself."*

If it is about toning and muscling up your body, the conversation that you have with yourself may go as follows: "I have always been in awe of the forgiving, elastic nature of my body. Over the years I have been a yo-yo dieter, and I have avoided most opportunities to exercise. My weight has fluctuated quite a bit, and yet my body remains relatively free of stretch marks. As I embrace this appreciation of my body, I am beginning to understand that I can create my life-long dream of having a toned and proportionally muscular body."

You are lining up your thoughts with your feelings. Perhaps you never thought of yourself as someone who would exercise, go to the gym, or lift weights. You now begin to ponder this idea with a new sense of confidence and enthusiasm.

For others, it will simply be about getting out and walking in the morning or evening on your own, or with a friend, to increase your level of fitness. Maybe you are someone who has wanted to do so your entire life, and you have found every excuse as to why you could not. Possibly you viewed something on television, or in a magazine, that inspired you to make a shift from the thinking about this desire to the actual consideration of taking action.

You are in the beginning stages of creating alignment with this desire. In time you will feel the effortlessness of heading out for a walk, or calling your friends and joining them in an activity which you have desired to do your entire life.

When we focus our attention on the things that we desire, we feel good. From that good-feeling place we have raised our vibration. Our vibration becomes our point of attraction for what we desire. What we think about is what we receive.

Once you understand this and wrap your mind around this universal law of attraction, you will become the powerful, deliberate creator that you came here to be.

Think about the way that you would like it to be, instead of the "way it is." What we think about is reflected accurately in the life that we are living. Change the thought and you will change your life.

THERE ARE ONLY TWO REASONS TO LOOK BACK

Sometimes people dread the idea of making changes, because they feel they will have to go back and dredge up old feelings and events.

Let's be very clear about this as far as we are concerned: there are only two reasons to revisit your past. The first reason is to revisit something that felt really good — and when you think about it in your now, it *still* makes you feel good. For example, think of a clear, loving and happy memory from any time in your life that makes you laugh and giggle. This would be a good memory to revisit as often as you can. If you find that this memory is triggering other memories which do not feel good, then this is not the memory to look back on.

The first reason to tap into an old memory is

to reactivate a good, joyful, and loving feeling. When we are able to isolate a loving, joyful memory from childhood, or a past relationship, and play only these thoughts and feelings over and over like a wonderful obsession, then they can help us to create a corrective emotional experience for ourselves. In time, we can begin to create a new understanding about this period of time in our lives, with our new thoughts and good feelings. We isolate, identify, and connect to only the loving, joyful parts of those times in our lives. In essence, we are recreating our own history for ourselves.

We have access to so many wonderful and not-so wonderful memories. Only pick the wonderful ones that create joy for you as you reflect back on them, and revisit them as often as possible. Think of it as if you were moving and only taking your best things with you. Leave the rest behind. Use every reflection of something in the past as a new, wonderful opportunity to connect yourself with yourself and feel good.

The second reason to look back is to clean up the residue of an old vibration that somehow you have unconsciously reactivated. For instance, you may have experienced friendships that were disappointing or unfulfilling at the time. You created thoughts and feelings around them that were less than joyful and oftentimes painful. You may think that you have left those kinds of relationships behind, because you are not consciously thinking about them. However, you might observe that your newer friendships produce the same unmet expectations, and those feelings of old become re-activated in your now.

Cleaning up the residue of an old vibration is an invaluable process that just takes a few minutes to do. It is important to identify if what you are feeling is in your now, or if it is reactivating something old. Ask yourself, "is this really happening now?"

Usually you are tapping into an old vibration that did not contribute to your balance and well-being. The recurring feeling is like a snag or a pebble in your shoe, and for some reason you keep coming back to it. Let it go.

It's like when you leave a room in disarray, walk away, and close the door—the disorder is still there. The disarray represents the disappointment, mistrust and unhappiness around the past situation. This technique provides an opportunity to go back and revisit the old feeling, and then replace it with a new one.

If you have a question about whether or not this is "old stuff," consider this: if the feeling is very strong, it is a good indicator that it is resonating from a place other than the here-

and-now. It is not possible that the current situation is creating this depth of feeling.

Once you identify that you have reactivated an old vibration, and you decide that you want to revisit and clean it up, it's like telling the story all over again. But this time, tell the version *that feels good to you.*

For example, as a teenager you may have felt awkward and felt rejection from the opposite sex. You may have experienced unrequited love and had an encounter that was painful. In your now, you may be struggling with relationships and undermining the possibility of having a happy and healthy partnership. You may have thought you walked away from that past situation, but you find yourself re-enacting it over and over again.

Here is your opportunity to go back and rewrite the story. Allow yourself to see it, feel it, and tell it, as you want it to be — you are attractive, you are desirable, and that secret crush had a crush on *you* first. This is a better-feeling story, and you have successfully cleaned up the vibration around this particular situation.

This is a gentle process, and you may want to continue to retell the story until it feels better, better, and finally best to you. Those good feelings will be reflected in your now.

If you are not ready to change your storyline at this time, and your focus is more about "the truth," then simply close the door and allow the disarray to remain. Whether you choose to go back and clean up the reactivated vibration— replacing it with something that feels better— or not, simply acknowledge it as a reactivation of an old vibration. This knowledge sets you free. You can never think of yourself as a victim of an old reactivated vibration again, because you now understand what you are reactivating and reacting to.

Let us look at another example. As a young adult,

you may have experienced some difficulty with your self-confidence and self-esteem. You are now an accomplished adult who works in a highly visible, professional setting. You are being considered for a promotion and are asked to make a presentation to a large group of colleagues. Then—*bam!*—it hits you like a ton of bricks; you suddenly feel paralyzed, unworthy, uncertain, and unclear.

This is a wonderful example of an old feeling that you have reactivated. Ask yourself, "does this have anything to do with my now?" The answer would most certainly be *no*.

Take a moment and go back and identify what this feeling is reminiscent of. And laugh, because this is clearly an old, reactivated vibration. Now let's take a few moments and clean it up, so that you can get on to your presentation and soon-to-be promotion.

Isolate the old feeling and re-frame it for

yourself. Remind yourself that young adult-hood is a time of questioning oneself and being more sensitive to the concerns of others. Remember your own concerns for yourself with a new understanding and appreciation.

Yes, it may have been difficult, awkward, and stressful, but from all that contrast you created a wonderful opportunity for yourself. Take pride in yourself for who you were then, and who you are now. Flash-forward to your now, and fly, birdie, *fly.*

We spend so much time cleansing our bodies, why not our vibration? Vibrational energy is everything. When we are not consciously creating, we leave little bits and pieces of our energy wherever we go and with whomever we encounter. It is important that we manage our own vibration at all times. It's just really great to know that, in a moment's time, we can go back and clean it up, and then be on our merry way.

Cleaning up your vibration around all kinds of things helps your life run smoothly and effortlessly.

Move along, move along, move along, and for goodness' sake, if you're going to choose to take that old piece of luggage, or vibration, with you, then lighten the load by changing the story so that you feel good carrying it.

ALLOWING

As we move through the world, the key to sharing our lives with other people happens with great success when we practice the concept of allowing. Allowing, for our purposes here, means remaining in your most connected state of being as you interface with the world that you live in. Allowing is a process that we must reclaim.

As children, we have very few judgments, prejudices, or points of view. However, children are keen observers. They remain in their state of well-being until the influence of family, parents, societal norms, and values lure them away from their inner knowing. Through our judgments about other people's behavior, we teach our children to make others "wrong" in order for them to believe that what they feel is "right."

Everyday, we ask people to change their behavior to make ourselves feel more comfortable. This very reaction—in other words, having a point of view about another's behavior—instantly takes us from a connected state to a disconnected state. We become dependent on another's behavior or actions so that we may feel good or happy. This is the antithesis of allowing.

If we believe or buy into the notion that we only have control over what we think about and how we feel, then we know that we cannot control another person's thoughts, actions, and feelings. This realization provides us with a wonderful opportunity to practice allowing. We remain in our own connected state as we allow others to do the same. Everybody gets to do what feels good and correct for themselves. And the clearer we become about what feels good to us, the easier it becomes to allow others to determine what feels good to them.

Allowing is counter-intuitive to what we have

been taught. We have come to believe that we are expected to develop opinions about other people's lives. This is propagated by the media. We speculate about celebrities and their love lives, colleagues in our work environment, and even what our neighbors are doing. This becomes the grounds for all manner of social interactions.

If we were to look at our life and focus on our own selves and what is right for us (and leave others to find what is right for them), then we would be happier, more productive, and have a greater ability to connect with ourselves and others.

If we were to live in a world where we did not have an opinion about another person's point of view, behavior, or how they looked or acted—that is, if we were able to remove all judgment—then it would free us to focus all of our energy on connection.

When you are truly clear about what you want for yourself, you are in a much better place to allow other people to do what they feel is right for themselves. If you are with your friends and find them participating in activities that do not feel good to you, it is best to remove yourself. To simply remove yourself will feel good, but to remove yourself without judgment will feel better and allow you to remain connected to yourself—this is allowing.

Love and allowing

How do you create a loving relationship with another? It is about allowing yourself to completely relax into who you are, and not asking your partner, children, or anyone you know to change who they are to make you feel better.

Creating a loving, intimate relationship

When we love ourselves, it is so easy to love those around us. Self-love, as we have said before, is our first true love. When we are in alignment with ourselves, we can create wonderful opportunities to attract the perfect partner.

Who is the perfect partner? It is different for everyone. From our place of alignment and a loving connection, we can begin to attract a loving partner into our experience. When we are in alignment, we tend to attract people into our life that complement the things we like about ourselves, even though they may be very different from us. The key to being in a successful, intimate, and loving relationship is to be in the state of allowing.

Allowing is different from tolerating. When you tolerate, you are "putting up" with people's differences. To allow is to embrace people's decision of who they want to be for themselves, without having to take their choice on.

When we look back on past intimate relation-ships, we begin to identify the things we would like to create for ourselves with another. As we sift through the contrast, we gain a new sense of clarity. Allowing occurs when we are connected to ourselves in understanding that others are not here to please us, or to make us feel better or worse about ourselves. One must do that for oneself.

With your new understanding, you might ask yourself "does familiar always feel best?" We often keep repeating the same kind of relationships.

But when we start to consciously choose how we want to move through the world, we find ourselves making new choices and being clearer about what we want for ourselves in a relationship with another. When you are in a successful, happy, and loving relationship, it feels good. When you love yourself, you don't want or need to change anyone or anything.

Allow yourself to create the loving relationship with yourself that you would like to create with another.

Children and Allowing

How do we co-create a loving relationship with our children, and allow them to stay tuned into who they truly are? Time and time again, we as parents want to direct our children to a place where they make what we perceive as good choices—but good for them or us? Coaching children inward allows them to know how they feel about something, not how *we* feel. They are then able to take responsibility for the outcome of their own experiences, instead of it being about our reaction to their behavior.

If we as parents could set our fears aside regarding our children's decisions, we would do them a great service. By simply asking children from the earliest time "what do you think?" and "how do you feel?" we allow and encourage children to look within and begin the process of feeling around with their intuition and inner knowing.

When teenagers ask about going to a party or going out with friends, instead of immediately telling them how you feel about them going to the party, ask them how *they* feel about going to the party. This gives them time to consider how the situation may feel for them.

Usually what occurs is that the parent says no, and then the entire process is about the child reacting to the parent's resistance with their own resistance. They may not have even wanted to attend the party, but now they do, and the entire issue becomes about their parents' reaction.

When we coach our children and young adults

inward, and remind them that they know what is best for themselves, we are providing the trust in them and encouraging them to trust themselves. They are then able to take responsibility for their own outcome — good or not so good.

Consider a teenager who asks if he or she can go to a party on a weekend night. Your first question might be "who is going to be at the party?" Instead, it could be, "That sounds fun. How do you feel about going to the party?" This gives the teen time to really ask himself or herself just that: how do *I* feel about going to the party?

The parents could then say, "You know you have really great instincts, and if this party seems like fun to you, then you should go. You know what is best for you. If something is not feeling comfortable to you at any point in the evening, call me and I will be happy to come pick you up."

That's a lot for a young adult to think about without the influence of the parents' point of view! However, in time they are *checking in* with themselves instead of *checking out*.

Reaction

When we react to something, we take a defensive or protective stance, because we are hearing or experiencing something that is not resonating with us in that moment. It is a learned, reflexive response that our culture has adopted. When we are in a situation where we perceive we are being slighted, attacked, or treated unjustly, then we often do not take the time to pause, to really hear, listen, and feel what the other person is saying. We meet thrust with thrust. Our mind and our body tenses. We push back and create resistance.

If you find yourself in this situation, then it might be a good time to say, "Let me think about that, and get back to you." You have immediately created an opening for yourself to hear what has been requested of you. You can then decide how—or if you even want—to respond to the situation. We often react quickly; because we think when we are asked something that we have to know the correct answer right away.

When you realize that you do not have to respond in the moment, it allows you to explore and consider the issue at hand. You can begin practicing this technique at once. As you begin to address these kinds of situations in a different way, you will take them less personally and ease into a better understanding of how you would like to respond.

When we hear and assimilate information without engaging our ego, we are better able to see, feel, and use that information to navigate the bigger picture. It no longer is about who is right or who is wrong, but becomes a neutral approach to a myriad of ideas that are being exchanged.

Allowing is a wonderful way to move about the world, because once you understand that you do not need to have a point of view, or take a stance on issues for anyone but yourself, you are free to openly receive and exchange information and ideas—in a way that you can truly hear and be heard. This does not mean you cannot have strong preferences, but it means that those preferences are for you and only you.

For some, allowing will take practice. For others, it only takes a moment to make a shift to this better-feeling place of allowing.

CHANGING YOUR STORYLINE

Our story is what we tell ourselves and others over and over, about who we are and what our situation is. It is like our mantra. Even as we are incessantly reciting our story, most of the time we are unaware of how we feel about it. Ask yourself, *how do you feel when you are telling your story?* Is your story working for you? Does it feel good?

If so, then keep telling it, because the life that you are living is a direct reflection of the story that you are telling, and it's all working well for you. If your story does not feel good to you when you are telling it, then it probably does not feel good to you as you are living it.

The beauty of this revelation is that at any time, in a moment's notice, you can change your storyline. You can recreate a small part of it, or create an entirely new story. This story feels good when you tell it, and feels good as you begin to live it. The new story is more about the way that you would like things to be, and less about the way that things are.

We are conditioned to tell the story that will give us the greatest audience. Most people key into the sympathy and drama of our story. Pay attention to how you feel when you are reciting your story. What is the vibrational tone? Sometimes it is not about the content, but the underlining essence of what is being said.

How is it that we become so invested in our story? We become comfortable and familiar with the tale we tell about our life. We feel the need to share "the hard truth" about ourselves. Oftentimes the story we tell ourselves and others creates what we perceive as sympathy and understanding. It feels as though the more drama we wrap around ourselves, the more attention we receive. The attention may feel good in the moment, but we may want to ask ourselves whether the story we are telling is truly a reflection of the life that we would like to be living.

We come to believe that our story is our life, when in actuality it is a reflection of the story that we are telling in the moment. Therefore, when you change your storyline you begin to change your life.

One of the tools in re-creating our story is a process called *re-framing*. We have spoken of shifting your focus, and this is another aspect of that. You will begin to identify and re-create your story in such a way that brings you joy and happiness every time you tell it. And then when you step into your story and live it, you will have regained your natural state of well-being.

Let's address a situation that we might choose

to re-frame. Your current storyline may be about how hard you work, and that you are not appreciated in your work environment.

Instead of saying how hard you work, you might want to re-frame the situation as "I am really good at what I do," "the company must think highly of me to give me so much autonomy," or "it is really great that I provide such a wonderful service." This is a powerful example of re-framing. The ease of this new storyline may provide a subtle shift in how you are feeling about your current situation.

It is important to find something to appreciate about your current situation. If you don't like your current position you might say, "I know that the contrast in this situation is providing me with the clarity of what I want in my next position," or "there is a wonderful new work opportunity that I am creating alignment with."

Initially you may feel some resistance around this conversation. The re-framing tool allows you to gently approach your current position of how you are feeling about it right now. It allows you to create an opening for change.

How would you like your current situation to be? Not "how it is," but how would you like it to be? This becomes your new question as you begin a dialogue with yourself about creating your new story. Remember you have the choice to create any and all aspects of your story.

These examples provide a new way of thinking about your current situation. The tone of the words you choose may give you a better feeling in your mind and your body. Remember, you may use re-framing at any time. Have fun with it.

THE PURPOSE OF OUR LIFE IS JOY

Joy is the emotion of great happiness, keen pleasure, and delight. It fills us with ecstatic pleasure and satisfaction.

There have been numerous studies which support and substantiate the evidence that when we are experiencing joy, creating joy, choosing joy, or sending thoughts and feelings of joy to another, we are releasing endorphins and changing the chemistry of our brain.

There is great value in the feeling of joy. Whether you tap into your own or someone else's joy, it raises your vibration. As you now understand, you have a choice of where you put your attention at any given moment. If you are wrestling with how you are feeling, pick a moment, person, place, or thing that infuses you with a good feeling. It could be the thought of a loved one, a pet, a beautiful place you have visited, or a picture you have seen. Think of it as literally plugging into a good-feeling thought.

Another way to experience joy is through the observation of others. Again, you are choosing where you put your attention. You might be in a grocery store and observe a loving interaction between a mother and child. You could be walking through the park and see friends laughing together, or lovers touching and caressing each other. The more you seek these lovely, joyful moments, the more you will observe them, and it will continue to add to the richness of your experience.

Laughter

"Sometimes just changing your face and your body language can create more space in your mind. Laughter is a real aid to bring about that spaciousness."
    –James Baraz, author of *Awakening Joy*

Laughter is a physical and mental expression of joy. It is a social lubricant. We often use laughter in moments when we are uncomfortable, and it helps us cross the threshold of that uncomfortable feeling and gain clarity.

Humor can be subjective, but laughter is a universal language. Laughter connects people with their humanity. It is uplifting and gives warmth. It improves the psychological well-being of people living through traumatic circumstances, such as wars and natural disasters. To laugh at a time when you are distressed is not to sidestep the emotional content, but to gain the clarity in order to make the experience productive.

Laughter is a great way to release psychic tension. When we re-frame something seemingly tragic or dramatic as humorous, we can then laugh at it. It doesn't become as big a deal. We are now able to move forward quickly with a renewed perspective. Laughter can provide a momentary pause from a stressful emotional situation. Set yourself free with laughter as you jump on everyone's joy with great pleasure.

Forgiveness is one of the keys to your own happiness. Compassionate feelings support a willingness to forgive. When we are able to forgive ourselves, we are able to forgive others. Forgiveness is a state of grace. It feels so good when we are at the giving and receiving end of it. Forgiveness is a bridge to love. Forgiveness is a release. When you can release the feelings of hurt, anger, and frustration that you may be carrying with you, and when you can let go of the self-condemnation, you will feel better and lighter.

The reason to forgive is for *you* to feel better. Forgiveness is an important process that brings peace to our soul, and harmony to our life. Forgiveness is not something we must do, but something we must allow to flow through us.

DAILY REMINDERS THAT YOU ALREADY KNOW

How This Book Came to Be

Embrace the contrast; for this is what gives us our clarity.

Making our transition from physical to non-physical is a beautiful thing. It is those who we leave behind that may temporarily lose their balance. Take comfort in knowing that *all is well*.

Your Inner Being

Ocean of light, sea of love, unceasing and completely unconditional; that would be your inner being!

I invite you to consider yourself first, for you are truly your own greatest resource!

If it feels good to you from your place of connection, then it must be good for you. Trust yourself! Who would know better than you what feels good for you?

All of our power lies in the ability to embrace the choices that we can make for ourselves about how we feel on a moment-to-moment basis, simply by consciously choosing what we are thinking about. We can only do this for ourselves! (Or not!)

Feel your way through your day. Trust yourself! Who would know better for you than you? Absolutely no one!

I invite you to become curious about the tone of your inner dialog that you are having with yourself on a daily basis. Are you having the loving conversations with yourself that you would like others to have with you?

I invite you to tap into your inner knowing first. This is where you will find the answers to your questions. You know, you always know!

Nourish yourself into connection!

On call 24/7, 365: that would be your inner being just waiting for you to tune in and be guided!

Our vibrational essence is emanated by how we *feel* about what we are saying and what we are doing. I invite you to step out of your head and *feel* your way through your day.

Selectively sift through each and every conversation, and only give your attention to that which feels good to you.

Shine that ever-loving light on you!

There are so many wonderful ways that we can nourish ourselves back into our feeling of connection! What will you choose for yourself today?

To become enlightened is to become connected with yourself, your inner being, and your inner knowing.

Tune in and embrace the most accessible, brilliant, all-knowing, free, and without-a-doubt-who-would-know-better-than-you resource: *yourself!*

We are truly our own greatest resource. Consider yourself first, who would know better for you than you?

Well-being is a connected state of being happy, healthy, and prosperous.

When our dominate intention is to *feel good*, we allow ourselves to be guided by our inner being. Our inner being is continually encouraging us to reach for the thought that feels better!

When we are able to turn down the volume of our mind chatter, we can begin to hear ourselves!

When we can become curious about ourselves, we are consciously opening up to ourselves in the most loving way. Gently, we are then able to find our way back to that good-feeling place of connection.

When we choose not to listen to our inner voice, we often find ourselves in situations that are less than desirable!

When we tune into our inner being—our inner knowing—we can then guide ourselves to where we are wanting to go. Trust yourself, you know. You always know!

When you ask (consciously or unconsciously), it is given every single time.

When you hook yourself up with yourself and allow yourself to feel the elation of connecting to your inner being, higher power, Christ consciousness, or whatever you want to call it, just know that you have the power to feel this good all of the time! It is choice. *Your choice.*

You are your own greatest resource, simply look within and believe. You know, you know, *you always know*.

Your inner being is calling you to a better feeling place 24/7, 365. The question is . . . *are you going?*

Your inner guidance is calling you!

Have a Love Affair with Yourself

What makes your heart flutter with joy?

Feel the love flow through you as you extend yourself unconditionally out into the world!

The most important opinion is the one that you have of yourself!

Above all stay open to love!

Create a long-term, beautiful and connected relationship with yourself!

Create the loving relationship with yourself that you would like to have with another.

I invite you to become more aware of the tone of every conversation that you are having with yourself. Are you streaming loving, soothing words of encouragement to yourself about yourself?

I invite you to create loving, internal conversations with yourself about yourself. No one else can do this for you but you. You are so worth it!

I invite you to give yourself the greatest gift of all, and this would be the gift of *self love!*

Imagine the freedom of not being dependent on what other people felt about us to feel good about ourselves? *Now that is true self love!*

It is all about self love!

It is all about the ever-loving, magnificent, vibrational essence of you!

Love, love, love, or more love? This is the question!

Nourish yourself with your conscious, focused, loving thoughts!

Self-love is our first true, big love.

Self-love is an intrinsic part of our nature. Our connection with our inner being is what returns us back to believing that sense of self-love.

Sometimes we simply need permission to redirect ourselves inward, back to the most important relationship, the one that we have with ourselves.

Teach through your loving and joyful connection to yourself first. Then, if you wish, allow yourself to unconditionally flow that magic to others.

The relationship that we have with ourselves is singularly the most important relationship that we will ever have!

The ultimate hook-up is when you redirect yourself inward to the connection that you have with yourself!

To feel good or to feel *really* good? This is the question!

Vibrationally speaking, keep it high!

When we are loving ourselves, it feels effortless to extend that love to those around us!

When we can create that loving, connected relationship with ourselves first— the relation-ship that we would like to have with another— we are then so easily able to attract that other connected, loving being into our experience. *Ah, co-creation at its finest!*

When you give yourself the gift of unconditionally loving yourself, you worry not about what anyone else is thinking about you!

When you love yourself, you are attracted to everyone, everywhere!

Alignment

I invite you to relax back into your natural state of well-being. From this balanced place of connection, everything feels good, as it should!

Emotions lead to action while reason leads to conclusions. Feel your way through your day.

Flowing from one amazing experience to the next. *Ah, that's life!*

Focus your attention solely on the parts of your life that please you. Why? Because you will feel good, and you will receive more of what pleases you. *A win-win all around!*

From our place of connection, it becomes so easy to set aside the drama, resistance and resentments as we allow ourselves to flow effortlessly from one magical moment to another!

It all begins with a conscious thought!

It is *never* about what you decide to do; it is *always* about how you feel about what you decide to do. *Why? Because inspired action is the only action!* And that's a fact, jack.

Nourish yourself into connection first. It is from this loving and connected place you may, if you choose, extend yourself to others unconditionally. This would be without any expectation or concern as to how you will be received. *Simply stated, you are extending yourself from a place of already feeling good.* You are not extending yourself to others in order to feel good.

Procrastination is a beautiful thing. It reminds us to pause and take our time to get into perfect alignment with any action before we take it. The outcome is without a doubt *sweet success* every single time!

Take responsibility for your own experience; manage your vibration at all times, and remember: there is nothing more important than feeling *good* — nothing!

We can easily tap into our inner knowing, inner guiding, and inner voice simply by consciously letting go of our ego, our fears, and then quieting our mind chatter. I invite you to trust yourself and allow yourself to relax into your own amazing internal guidance system.

Whatever we are expecting to happen, happens every single time — no exceptions!

When we allow ourselves to let go of all resentments, we are freed up to embrace the *long view*. The long view is the vision of our own individual life. Create alignment with your vision, and let the magic begin!

When you place your attention on only that which pleases you, you feel good. And when you feel good, you have raised your vibration, and when you have raised your vibration (because you feel good), *it is like being on cloud nine all of the time!*

Appreciation

Choose to place your attention on the beauty, pleasure, and joy of every single moment.

That's right, it's all supposed to feel good. Every minute of every single day!

Allow yourself to seek out the beauty, joy, love, and laughter that this day has to offer. It is all around you! Can you see it? *Can you feel it?*

May this beautiful day begin with a conscious thought that sets the tone for feeling good!

When we choose to feel good we raise our vibration, and when our vibration is high, we feel connected to ourselves, and when we feel connected to ourselves—well glory be, we feel connected to everyone everywhere!

And now let us bask in the love and appreciation, abundance and joy, and beauty and pleasure that we are—from this moment forward, wishing to create for ourselves with our focused thoughts and good feelings! *Let the manifestations begin.*

Appreciation feels like a blissful state of connection!

I am feeling so much love and appreciation for all of the wonderful people that I have attracted into my life.

I invite you to bask in a memory, feeling, or thought that allows you to feel really good. This is a luxury that we can all afford!

I invite you to step out of your head and into your life. *Feel your way through your day.*

Life is a magnificent feast for the senses. *Ah*, and it all feels *so good*!

May every moment of your day be a wonderful excuse to feel good!

The greatest investment is the one that you

make in yourself. From there you are ready to embrace the world!

This life of mine—*well, it is nothing short of amazing!*

When we immerse ourselves in a state of appreciation and flow—*these loving thoughts to ourselves and others*—it feels amazing!

With deep appreciation, I am basking in the beauty, pleasure, and joy of the wonderful life that I have joyously created.

Deliberate Creation

A suggested mantra for the day: *everything is going my way!*

Consider the outrageous as you consciously create your day!

Create your every desire, one thought at a time. Have a *fan-fucking-tastic day!*

Daydream your way into creating the life that you are wanting for yourself! *Go ahead, try it.* It is oh so fun and it really works.

Deliberate creation or creating by default? You choose. This decision is always by choice. *Your choice!*

Desire is the jumping off point for everything that you manifest!

Did you know that when you are daydreaming, you are doing some powerful manifesting. *What a day for a daydream!*

Did you know that you have the freedom to choose how you would like to feel every moment of the day. No one can make us feel anything. *It is all choice, our choice!*

Empower yourself with this little piece of knowledge: *we create our own experiences with our thoughts.*

Feeling good is a lovely option. It is all choice, your choice.

I invite you to allow any contrast that you may experience throughout your day to become a lovely opportunity for you to check back in with yourself and become curious, in this moment, about your own vibrational frequency.

I invite you to consciously create a good feeling within yourself.

I invite you to consciously create your day, *one good feeling at a time.*

I invite you to deliberately create some time for yourself today.

If we can buy into the notion that we are 100 percent responsible for the content of our thoughts, then we can begin to consider that with those thoughts we have the most amazing opportunity to create a wonderful reality for ourselves.

If you buy into the notion that we create with our thoughts; what will you be thinking about today?

In this moment, I choose to create with my thoughts an amazing day for myself!

Intoxicated by the knowing that anything and everything is possible!

It is all about feeling good one thought at a time!

It is all about the joyous deliberate creation— *now that's intoxicating.*

It only takes a moment to make a shift in your thinking and create a better feeling for yourself!

Oh the joy of deliberate creation!

Personal freedom is attained when we take responsibility for what we think about and how we feel.

Take a moment to deliberately create this day for yourself!

The people, animals, situations, and opportunities that we attract into *(and out of)* our lives become a wonderfully accurate indicator as to how we are vibrating at every moment. *Law of Attraction sorts it out every single time.*

The universe always has your back. The question is, *are you a cooperative component?*

We are 100 percent responsible for how we feel. This means that we have the choice to feel good every moment of every day. Or not. *It is choice, our choice!*

We only have control over three things: what we choose to think about, how we choose to feel, and how we choose to direct our thoughts and feelings to create an amazing life for ourselves!

What you think about is what you receive, so direct your thoughts accordingly!

When we realize that we are 100 percent responsible for our own happiness, and we redirect ourselves back to the most important relationship—the one that we have with ourselves—we let everyone else off the hook, because now we understand that there is only one source for our happiness, *and that is ourselves.* It becomes an individual choice. We cannot choose happiness for another.

You are the director, and the universe is the manager!

There Are Only Two Reasons to Look Back

Surprise, you do not have to look back in order to move forward!

Allowing

When we allow what others are thinking

and feeling to throw us off of our game, we are truly giving away our power.

We can only create an amazing life for ourselves. We do not have the ability to create for another. We can, however, live our amazing life and become the example of all that is possible.

Food for thought: if the only thing that we did differently each day was to substitute the word *"and"* for the word *"but,"* then we could make a significant shift in our vibration.

I invite you to leave behind all of your judgments of self and others as you move about the world today. *Let the magic begin!*

Leave your ego at the opening of every door that you walk through, and you will create a wonderful opportunity to connect with the world!

The most important opinions are the ones that we have about ourselves. I invite you to join your inner being and *embrace yourself with love and kindness.*

Visionary or reactionary? How are you directing your life with your thoughts?

When we allow ourselves to remove all judgment and embrace the world with an open loving heart, *it feels so good!*

When we are nourished emotionally, physically, and, for some, spiritually, we can extend ourselves in such a loving and unconditional way!

When we create a loving connection with ourselves and then allow ourselves to relax into that feeling of connection, our ego falls away. *What a powerful way to move about the world!*

When we have *clarity* about the choices that we are making for ourselves, we care not about the choices that others are making for themselves. It is only when we do not have clarity for ourselves that, all of a sudden, we have a point of view about what everyone else is thinking, saying, and doing!

When you love yourself, you do not want to change anyone or anything about another!

Changing Your Storyline

Change your thoughts, and you will change your life!

Consider this — the life *that you are living* is an accurate reflection of what you are thinking and feeling. And, most of all, *how you are vibrating.*

Most often, within every problem lies a wonderful opportunity!

The life that you are living is a reflection of the thoughts that you are thinking. *Change your thoughts and you will change your life.* Only you can do for this for yourself!

The Purpose of Our Life is Joy

Choose joy!

And just when you think that it does not get better than this — guess what? *It gets even better!* Why? *Because the better it gets, the better it gets!*

Exuding joy and well-being to the point that it becomes *contagious*: a world-wide pandemic will do!

Feel for the *pleasure* in every moment!

Forgiveness is a bridge to love.

Forgiveness is an important process that brings peace to our soul and harmony to our life. Forgiveness is not something we must do, but something we must allow to flow through us.

Forgiveness is one of the keys to our own happiness.

How much pleasure, beauty, and joy will you be creating for yourself today?

Humor can be subjective, but laughter is a universal language.

Immerse yourself in the beauty, pleasure, and joy that surrounds you! It is all around you! Can you see it? *Can you feel it?*

Isn't it wonderful when we give ourselves the time to ponder something for the pleasure, curiosity, and *sheer joy of it?*

It is all about the beauty, pleasure, and endless amounts of joy!

Joy, joy and more joy! There have been numerous studies which support and substantiate evidence that when we are experiencing joy, creating joy, choosing joy, or sending thoughts and feelings of joy to another, we are in fact releasing more endorphins and changing the chemistry of our brain.

It's all about the *joy!*

Joyful expansion to the next wonderful endeavor, *and laughing all the way!*

Laugh your way through your day. Why? *Because it feels so good!*

Laughing and laughing and laughing and laughing, and it feels so good! It is going to be a *great fucking day!*

On a 24/7, 365 *vibrational* high!

On that 24/7, 365 pleasure trip of life!

Set yourself free with laughter as you jump on everyone's joy with great pleasure!

Sometimes we worry that if we remain in our connected state of joy for too long that we will lose our edge and not be as productive. This is not the case. We are actually *more productive,* as every idea and thought and action flows effortlessly through us. *When work feels like joy, you know you have it right!*

We cannot be too happy, healthy, abundant, joyful, or have too much pleasure in our life. I believe that we can choose to feel good all of the time!

What is your greatest *joy?* Pleasure, beauty, and joy! That's what I am talking about 24/7.

When your dominant intention is to feel good all of the time, you practice reaching for the better-feeling thought enough times that it becomes second nature. There is nothing more important than feeling good, *nothing!*

What is your greatest *pleasure?*

REFLECTIONS

This section is for your personal reflections and notes.

Reflections 150

Reflections 152

ABOUT THE AUTHORS

Jamie

Jamie Lerner lives and breathes the teachings of Abraham (Esther and Jerry Hicks). She is on what she calls her "third life." She has co-created a beautiful family with her successful and dynamic husband. She has received her MSW from Loyola University, and went on to create a wonderful, thriving, private psychotherapy practice. And she has traveled the world, exploring all types of spiritual healing modalities.

As a therapist, she continues to explore the many avenues of maintaining a balanced and happy connection. She has developed what she refers to as an integrative approach to well-being. Jamie Lerner is masterful in her ability to assist clients in re-creating a loving relationship with themselves. She invites you to visit her website, www.jamie-lerner.com, to contact her and learn more about it.

She is also a passionate, amateur adult equestrian rider on the AA horse show circuit. She has an insatiable appetite for pleasure, beauty, and joy; and often refers to herself as a true "pleasure junkie."

Lauren

Lauren Targ was born and raised in Highland Park, Illinois. She has worked in the theater as an actor, director and writer. She spent several years in the film business working as an art director. Teaching since high school, she spent many years developing programming and curriculum for inner city youth working on playwriting, acting and filmmaking. Her art installations have been shown in galleries and museums around the country. Her most recent work comprises a collaborative on-going audio piece entitled, "The Crush Project" (www. crushproject.org). She was also Director of Video for the highly visible Crown Fountain in Millennium Park on the famous North Michigan Avenue's Magnificent Mile in Chicago, Illinois.

She is trained in many healing techniques and is a certified Reiki master healer. Her natural knack for counseling, healing and motivating led her to her current positions teaching and advising at Columbia College Chicago. She earned her B.A. in English and Creative Writing from Lake Forest College, and an M.F.A. in Interdisciplinary Arts from Columbia College Chicago.

LaVergne, TN USA
07 March 2010
175192LV00001B/1/P